THE ZOO
YOU NEVER GNU

Books by Ben Milder

Poetry

The Good Book Says . . . : Light Verse to Illuminate
  the Old Testament   (1995)

The Good Book Also Says . . . : Numerous Humorous Poems
  Inspired by the New Testament   (1999)

Love Is Funny, Love Is Sad   (2002)

The Zoo You Never Gnu: A Mad Menagerie of Bizarre Beasts
  and Birds   (2004)

Medical

The Fine Art of Prescribing Glasses Without Making
  a Spectacle of Yourself   (1979)

History

On the Shoulders of Giants: A History of Ophthalmology
  at Washington University   (1999)

THE ZOO YOU NEVER GNU

A Mad Menagerie
of Bizarre Beasts and Birds

Poems by

Ben Milder

Illustrations by

Amour Krupnik

TIME BEING BOOKS
POETRY IN SIGHT AND SOUND

An imprint of Time Being Press
St. Louis, Missouri

Time Being Books®
10411 Clayton Road
St. Louis, Missouri 63131

Time Being Books® is an imprint of Time Being Press®, St. Louis, Missouri

Time Being Press® is a 501(c)(3) not-for-profit corporation.

Time Being Books® volumes are printed on acid-free paper, and binding materials are chosen for strength and durability.

ISBN 1-56809-093-5 (paperback)

Library of Congress Cataloging-in-Publication Data:

Milder, Benjamin, 1915–
    The zoo you never gnu : a mad menagerie of bizarre beasts and
  birds / Ben Milder ; illustrated by Amour Krupnik.— 1st ed.
      p. cm.
    ISBN 1-56809-093-5 (pbk. : alk. paper)
     1. Animals—Poetry. I. Krupnik, Amour. II. Title.

  PS3563.I37159Z66 2004
  811'.54—dc22

                                                      2003025334

Illustrations by Amour Krupnik
Book design and typesetting by Sheri Vandermolen

Manufactured in the United States of America

First Edition, first printing (2004)

Acknowledgments

I do not envy the role of the publisher. Bringing to fruition a book that is the joint effort of two very individual individuals — poet and artist — is akin to a feat of legerdemain. The publisher sits, often with his head in his hands, using his Solomonic wisdom to resolve the inevitable problems. When his hands are free, one is furiously operating an abacus, the other holding a bottle of aspirin, as he works to make the creative team come to terms with reality.

So, it is with admiration that I thank the people at Time Being Books for their efforts: Jerry Call, managing editor, Sheri Vandermolen, editor in chief, and Trilogy Brodsky, office manager. Also, I express my gratitude to the illustrator, Amour Krupnik, and to fellow poet and fine friend Louis Daniel Brodsky.

This "zoo" is lovingly dedicated to my grandchildren.

May they never weary of meeting their fellow travelers,
with whom they share this planet.

Contents

THE ZOO
YOU NEVER GNU

A Word from the Author

At your local zoo, you have long been acquainted with the elephant, the zebra, and the chimpanzee. They are old friends. But what of the xiphias, the hackee, the zebu, and the urubu? It should come as no surprise that we share mother earth with a strange, exotic collection of inhabitants.

In this volume, you will encounter a goodly number of these unusual animals. You will meet them in the form of a poetic palindrome, with creatures having names ranging from A to Z and back, from Z to A. You will learn something of the habits and idiosyncrasies of these animals. This book is also an invaluable tool for crossword-puzzle fanatics.

Agouti

The agouti is somehow related
To the guinea pig, it has been stated,
      But it isn't as cute —
      And much bigger, to boot.
As a pet, it is much overrated.

The agouti's as big as the rabbit,
And it moves so fast that you can't grab it.
      Without begging your pardon,
      It can chew up your garden,
Which agoutis are prone to inhabit.

As those creatures lay waste to your flowers
And your world outlook rapidly sours,
      Though it may seem self-serving,
      We take heart in observing
That those agoutis are yours and not ours.

Burro

An ass is the same as a donkey,
And a donkey resembles a burro.
But you wouldn't know one from the other
Without being somewhat more thorough.

There's the wild ass (the female's a "jenny,"
While the male ass is known as a "jack"),
And the donkey's an ass that was tamed
By Egyptians, some six thousand years back.

Now, burros are just little donkeys.
They ride them in old Mexico.
Just hop aboard, put them in motion,
And they'll take you wherever you go.

So, if gasoline prices skyrocket
And being prompt is a sine qua non,
You can do your commuting by burro.
Just be sure you start out before dawn.

Camelopard

If my parents were camelopards, I wonder what I'd be.
It's obvious that I would have to be some sort of mammal,
But what I'd really be would be a mystery to me.

Would I be more a leopard, or would I be mostly camel,
An animal with two large, hairy humps atop my spine,
Or would I be a dromedary? (Would one hump be ample?)

On the other hand, if I were mostly leopard, in design,
Like other leopards, I would be the fleetest of the fleet.
I'd roam the veld, in Africa; the meadows would be mine.

But I guess I'd be just like my dad, perched on the catbird seat.
I'd really be the tallest mammal, there is no denyin',
With a neck so long you'd need a ladder to inspect my teeth.

I may look awkward, like my parents, but folks don't abhor us.
I'm a very special mammal, not some freak that's half-and-half.
I'm the center of attraction at the circus. Folks adore us.

Neither camel nor a leopard, but I make the children laugh.
So, I look in my thesaurus, which is sitting there before us,
And I find there's no camelopard. I'm really a giraffe.

Dugong

Why is it when we think of mammals
Mostly common, some exotic,
We assume that they all live on land?
Many are aquatic.

The sea cow is one example,
And the walrus is a mammal, too.
There's the manatee, of which you've heard,
And the dugong, just to name a few.

Though the manatee and dugong
Are genetically synonymous,
We often read of manatees,
While the dugong stays anonymous.

The dugong's native habit
Is usually Australian,
Where he lives on things like sea grass,
Which each dugong munches daily on.

But don't pity the dugong.
Though his habitat's aquarian,
He is likely to outlive you,
'Cause his diet's vegetarian.

dugong: an aquatic, herbivorous mammal that is distinguished from the manatee by a bilobate tail resembling that of a whale

Eelworm (Vinegar Eel)

As these couplets will reveal,
The eelworm's not an eel.
What is more, it's not enormous;
Au contraire, it's vermiformous.

Now, if you are so inclined,
You can find worms of this kind
Congregated, in a bunch,
Among the flora, having lunch

In your supermarket's greens,
Where they linger, sight unseen,
Until, at last, they come to rest in
Both your small and large intestine.

And unless I am mistaken,
Very shortly, you'll be makin'
Many trips obligatory
To the nearest lavatory.

Other eelworms may be fated
To end up marinated,
In which case, you might just view it
Lifeless in a vinegar cruet,

A nematode which lies there, placid,
Floating in acetic acid.

Fer-de-lance

If, on bivouac, with troops, you should chance
To meet up with the feared fer-de-lance,
After just one quick glance,
That is one circumstance
When you'd beat a retreat, not advance.

fer-de-lance: a large, extremely venomous pit viper found in Central and South America

Gnu

The gnu, the gnu —
It's an antelope, true,
But you haven't a clue
How to say the word "gnu."

Don't despair; don't feel blue.
There are other folks who
May be in the same stew;
That includes experts, too.

Is it "nyu," as in "view,"
Or just "nu," as in "boo"?
Is the "g" silent, too,
Like the "k" is in "knew"?

It's undoubtedly true
There'd be no big to-do
If etymologists knew
How to say the word "gnu."

So, what else is gnu?

gnu: any of several rather large but compact and blocky African antelopes having a large head like that of an ox, short mane, and a long and flowing tail, with horns, in both sexes, that curve downward and outward

Hackee

The hackee is a little squirrel,
But could it also be
The weekend golfer's little ball
That sits upon a tee?

Just think, a donor's largesse
Always goes to the donee,
And the recipient of honors
Now becomes the honoree.

If a golfer's score for eighteen holes
Is one hundred thirty-three,
Is that golfer not the hacker
And the ball not the "hackee"?

So, the hackee is a golf ball,
But it pays to be discreet.
I don't think I would swing at it
If it had four little feet.

hackee: a chipmunk (a small, striped American squirrel)

Ibex

I wish I were an ibex, European or north Asian.
I'd join my friends up near the timberline.
I'd munch on shrubs and juniper as often as I please
And nibble on some wine-producing vines.

I'd be the king of ibexes, as I'd lope through the alps;
I'd disport myself in manner that is regal.
I'd particularly relish daily gamboling through the gorse,
Because gambling, in my home state, is illegal.

ibex: a wild goat in the high mountain areas of the Old World; it is believed
to be the progenitor of the domestic goat

Javelina

Let's all do the javelina!
Is that some dance, like boogaloo?
If so, what is it doing
In a crossword-puzzle zoo?

With a name like "javelina,"
A word that's so euphonious,
You might conclude that it's a song,
But that, too, is erroneous.

Javelina is a small wild pig,
Which you'd think no one loves,
But it has a useful role on earth —
In this case, leather gloves.

javelina: a peccary (a more or less nocturnal, gregarious wild swine); the collared, or the white-ribbed, peccary is sometimes used to make leather gloves

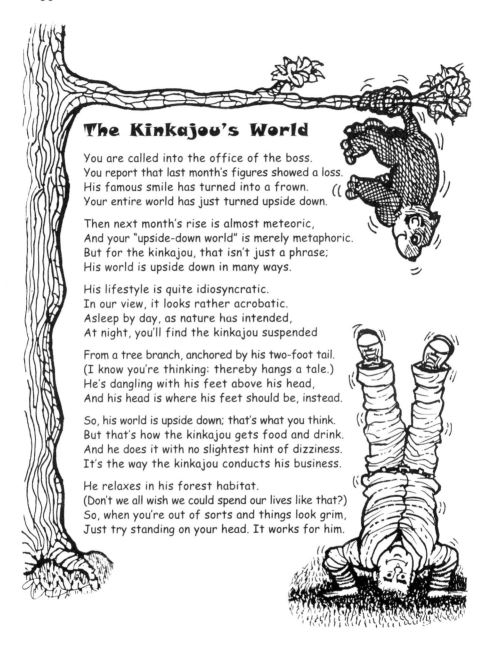

The Kinkajou's World

You are called into the office of the boss.
You report that last month's figures showed a loss.
His famous smile has turned into a frown.
Your entire world has just turned upside down.

Then next month's rise is almost meteoric,
And your "upside-down world" is merely metaphoric.
But for the kinkajou, that isn't just a phrase;
His world is upside down in many ways.

His lifestyle is quite idiosyncratic.
In our view, it looks rather acrobatic.
Asleep by day, as nature has intended,
At night, you'll find the kinkajou suspended

From a tree branch, anchored by his two-foot tail.
(I know you're thinking: thereby hangs a tale.)
He's dangling with his feet above his head,
And his head is where his feet should be, instead.

So, his world is upside down; that's what you think.
But that's how the kinkajou gets food and drink.
And he does it with no slightest hint of dizziness.
It's the way the kinkajou conducts his business.

He relaxes in his forest habitat.
(Don't we all wish we could spend our lives like that?)
So, when you're out of sorts and things look grim,
Just try standing on your head. It works for him.

kinkajou: a nocturnal, arboreal, carnivorous mammal inhabiting Mexico and Central and South America; it is about three feet in length, with a slender body, long, prehensile tail, large, lustrous eyes, and yellowish-brown fur

Lemming

The European lemming has a bent for mass migration,
Which strikes me as a most eccentric sort of avocation.
At certain times, those lemmings head directly for the water,
A ritual that ends up in a form of wholesale slaughter.

Just suppose that you're a lemming, at your annual convention.
Your leader wields his gavel, saying, "Now, let's pay attention.
Although we're only rodents, we are still 'birds of a feather.'
It's time we headed for the sea, so let's all stay together.

"Let's show the world, once more, that we are just one big community
And demonstrate, for all to see, our vaunted lemming unity.
It's a test of lemming manhood, so let none of us forsake it.
Just wade right in. If you can't swim, it's permissible to fake it.

"As usual, we're front-page news as we pursue our notion
Of marching, en masse, to the shore and then into the ocean.
Although we're little rodents, with short tails and fuzzy feet,
The entire world looks on, as our immersion is complete."

But little lemming, what about your own long-held ambition
To pass the bar exam or graduate as a physician?
If running with the herd is, sadly, one of your proclivities,
You'll be just one more rat that's drowned as part of the festivities.

What happens to those lemmings ought to be some sort of lesson
That not thinking for yourself is apt to be somewhat depressing.
So, you must have the fortitude to leave the family nest
And forgo the opportunity to drown like all the rest.

There's a moral to the lemmings' fate, which should be quite transparent.
The behavior of those lemmings, you'll agree, is incoherent.
So, don't go near the water, you have often heard it said.
If you make your own decisions, you won't end up very dead.

lemming: a small, short-tailed, furry-footed rodent; the European species is
notable for its recurrent mass migration, which often continues into the sea,
where vast numbers of the animal drown

Matamata

Matamata, whatsa matta?
How come you no pull your neck in?
Maybe you got neck arthritis
Or just lazy bones, I reckon.

Other turtles, they more savvy.
When in danger, they just hide.
Soon as they see trouble coming,
Pull their heads and necks inside.

I worry 'bout you, matamata.
Maybe one time you too reckless.
You no see the hunter coming,
Maybe end up with one neck less.

matamata: a weak-jawed, long-neck turtle; one of a family of "sideneck" turtles

Noctiluca (*Lampyris noctiluca*)

The firefly, or the glowworm, as we are wont to call it,
Comes with built-in flashlight (clearly, we did not install it).
As the firefly twinkles in the dusk, about our patio,
It seems at peace within its world. But little does it know
That the luminescence in its tail is garnering attention,
Which, if fireflies all had ESP, would cause some apprehension.

You see, it's destined for a fate that's mightily unpleasant,
All because, unhappily, its tail is phosphorescent.
Kids today, with nets, seize every firefly within reach
Then sell them at the going rate, of just one penny each,
To biochemists, who will promptly amputate their glow
And convert it into enzymes, which will net a lot more dough.

So, when you see those little fireflies twinkling on the premises,
Bow your heads in prayer, because researchers are their nemesis —
A requiem for fireflies who, though innocent, are fated
To have their glowing derrieres, for science, amputated.

Okapi

One day, a small okapi met up with a tall giraffe.
The okapi said, "Hi, cousin. It would seem that we're related."
The giraffe looked at the little mammal and began to laugh.
"To hint we're kith and kin would be to grossly overstate it.

"How could you be my cousin? You're more like a little ox.
The thought of common heritage just strikes me as ironic.
A giraffe with stubby neck like yours would be a paradox.
Folks would likely think of you as just oxymoronic."

The okapi drew himself up to his twenty-four inch height.
"I've always lived in Zaire, with enough food to get by on.
You think that just because you're taller you are also bright?
But we're cousins, though it's one thing we don't see eye to eye on."

okapi: a mammal closely related to the giraffe but somewhat smaller than an ox, with a relatively short neck, reddish-chestnut body, and upper legs ringed with cream and purplish black

Pangolin

On our safari trip, last year,
While looking for a souvenir,
You saw an oddball critter up ahead.
That's what you aimed your camera at,
Then asked the tour guide, "What was that?"
"Oh, that was just a pangolin," he said.

The creature had a funny nose,
Almost as big as Cyrano's —
A stranger in the Western Hemisphere.
I guess it didn't take baths daily,
Because its body was so scaly,
But a most unusual travel souvenir.

So, we unleashed our money clip
For that memento of our trip —
A pangolin as our own household pet.
Canned pet foods he didn't like,
So he went on a hunger strike,
And we took him off to see the local vet.

"Doc, our Pangolin cavorts
At family soirees of all sorts,
But it's clear he doesn't care for Uncle Pete.
Yet when Aunt Mathilda shows up,
He really gets his nose up;
He's excited, and he nibbles on her feet.

"What's going on here with our pet?
He seems to scorn old Pete, and, yet,
Aunt Mathilda — he just cannot wait to meet her.
Why are you laughing, doctor vet?"
"Your pango's not a household pet.
The pangolin's an African *anteater*!"

pangolin: an African edentate mammal with large, reddish-brown, imbricated
scales, feeding chiefly on ants; somewhat resembling the American anteater

Quagga

Said the donkey to the zebra, "You're a funny-looking horse.
You look just like a barber pole with feet."
Replied the zebra to the donkey, "You look even worse.
You're as colorless and dull as Irish peat."

And the donkey came back: "It is clear that you were misdesigned
By someone who was blind or astigmatic.
You're certainly a quadruped that is one of a kind.
That guy was 'round the bend,' some weird fanatic."

Then they thought about vendettas and said, "Hey, we're getting older.
Let's devise some sort of compromise design.
If the zebra's stripes were limited to just the head and shoulder
And the rest of it were plain, that would be fine.

"We would be a new addition to our quadruped zoology.
Let's experiment and see how it comes out."
Though this poet must omit the sex details of the technology,
Take my word; that's how the quagga came about.

quagga: an extinct wild ass of southern Africa, related to the zebra but which was brown, with a white tail and white legs and stripes only on its head and neck and the front part of its body, unlike the zebra, which has black and white stripes all over its body

What's a Roach?

In last night's crossword puzzle, I confess that I was stumped
By clues that were, to say the least, confusing:
"Something you can step on or consume or even smoke,"
In just five letters. It was not amusing.

Something I could step on? It could be a household pest
Roaming freely in our attics and our cellars,
The most despised of insects. Could that clue refer to "roach,"
Anathema to inner-city dwellers?

Of course! It must be "roach." It has five letters and is squashable.
But that isn't something one would choose to eat,
Except in countries where they can be purchased chocolate-coated
And considered, by the natives, quite a treat.

The "roach" is also a large fish, as much as ten feet long.
It is not an entrée for the epicure.
If roach is on the menu and it's moving, be aware:
It is not the trendy café's plat du jour.

But the puzzle's clues required that it be something you can smoke
As well as under foot and a comestible,
And "roach" is just a street name for a marijuana butt,
Which is smokable, illegal, and detestable.

If, in the proper squares, you entered R-O-A-C-H
And you put each letter in its proper niche,
We'll concede that you're a maven on the subject of the roach.
But that knowledge isn't apt to make you rich.

Skink

If a wizard found a lizard in a blizzard
And he cut the lizard up, from A to izzard,
Would the wizard who had scissored
The poor unhappy lizard
Make a meal of it or simply eat the gizzard?

But just suppose the lizard were, in fact, a skink
(That's a *skink* and not a *skunk* — it doesn't stink),
A little lizard with no malice
(By name, *Scincus officinalis*),
Would the wizard from a lizard like this shrink?

Would the wizard, from the premises, now slink
If he thought it was a skunk and not a skink?
Would he likely flee, in terror,
From a simple spelling error,
Pulling back the lizard's gizzard from the brink?

skink: any of a family of mostly small pleurodont lizards that have small scales

Tapir

It's one of God's works, and we're loath to malign it,
But the MIT faculty didn't design it.
It's graced with a snout which no one could call scanty.
It calls to one's mind the late Jimmy Durante.

But much more bizarre to the average viewer,
Each front foot has four toes, each hind foot one fewer.
That poses a problem well nigh insurmountable,
For which one can't hold the poor tapir accountable.

With digits arranged in such strange combinations,
He runs into trouble with most calculations.
If he counts on his fingers, he can't use the decimal,
So his knowledge of math must be infinitesimal.

Let's look at the human and tapir gray matter.
It's plain that the former has more than the latter,
But don't waste your pity, for when you consider it,
The tapir's well off, even though he's less literate.

He doesn't pay taxes and has no pollution.
He isn't caught up in the sex revolution.
He doesn't need things like the decimal system.
And it is quite obvious he hasn't missed 'em.

He manages quite well with just fourteen toes,
Though why he is made that way, God only knows!

tapir: a large ungulate found in Central and South American, the Malay
Peninsula, and Sumatra, with a sparsely haired body, a short, mobile
proboscis, a rudimentary tail, stout legs; chiefly nocturnal

Urus

The urus is a mammal, the zoologists inform us.
It is said to be a horned wild ox, but that should not alarm us,
Although the thought of such a beast is likely to repel us.
We learn the urus is extinct; at least that's what they tell us.

Since the experts all assure us that the urus is no more,
We can just relax and have no further worries on that score.
It's true that from the Ice Age, those wild oxen roamed Eurasia.
Still, there's one thing about them that is certain to amaze you:

They did not really disappear. No, they did not skedaddle.
They evolved, eight thousand years ago, into domestic cattle.
If nature had not so ordained and the urus still roamed free,
Restaurants would serve up urus steaks — but not to me.

Imagine chasing a wild ox or others of that ilk
And trying to get close enough to get a quart of milk.
The only cheese available would have to come from goats.
And what would we use, at breakfast time, to drown our Quaker Oats?

Where would we get the whipped cream for our cream puffs and éclairs
And the custards, necessary for prize-winning *boulangers*,
And important things like calcium, to supplement our diet?
If dairy cows did not exist, would uruses supply it?

To sum up: if the urus had not long since been deceased
And the hordes of those wild oxen had continued to increase,
The world would be the poorer if there were no bovine dairy.
How would we get along without our nightly Ben & Jerry?

urus: also called aurochs; a kind of extinct wild ox, the ancestor of present-day domestic cattle

Vireo

To rouse me from my slumber,
I'm assaulted, without warning,
By the tintinnabulation
Of my alarm clock every morning.

So, I bought myself a rooster,
Which crowed daily since I got it.
But it crowed so loud and early
That an irate neighbor shot it.

To the world of electronics
I now turned — I bought a stereo.
But then I couldn't program it,
So I bought a bird, a vireo

(A bird whose dulcet melodies
Outshone the nightingale and wren),
To rouse me gently every day,
Unlike my rooster or Big Ben.

Now, I waken, in good spirits,
To my vireo's "cheep, cheep."
But its music is so soothing
That it puts me back to sleep!

vireo: a small, insectivorous American passerine bird, noted for the beauty
of its singing

Widgeon

Though your expertise with birds is just a smidgeon
And you cannot tell a widgeon from a pigeon,
You needn't feel that you must make apology
If you are not well versed in ornithology.
The widgeon is a kind of duck that's found
In freshwater areas, where they abound.

The pigeon is a curse upon society.
Its unwanted droppings give it notoriety.
The bombardment, by the pigeon, of its waste
Unhappily is frequently misplaced
And falls upon your patio or garden,
Without so much as "Oops! I beg your pardon."

Homeowners would have no more pigeon wars,
And they wouldn't have to wear a hat outdoors
If, instead of forays by the unclean pigeon,
They were visited by something like the widgeon.
In size between a mallard and a teal,
The widgeon's not enough to make a meal.

Though nowhere to be found on any lists
Of endangered species, the idea persists
That while the pigeon is despised — not unexpected —
The widgeon, in our view, should be protected,
For most people find the widgeon much more pleasant
Than the pigeon, which, alas, is omnipresent.

So let's join up with the WPS*
And save those widgeons that are in distress.
Be vocal! Join our widgeon demonstration!
And don't forget to make a large donation.

*WPS: Widgeon Protective Society

Xenarthra

Xenarthra is a mammal of the order Edentata,
Which gets along without a single tooth.
Like all anteaters, this one seems to thrive on little ants.
I know that may sound odd, but it's the truth.

If you're thinking of acquiring a xenarthra as a pet
And you yearn to cuddle up with one, perchance,
You'd do well to start an ant farm. It is sure to fill the bill,
To keep this family pet well stocked with ants.

Of course, your friends will shun all invitations to your home,
And so will Uncle Harry and Aunt Martha.
Once they've had the fun of picking ants out of their clothes,
They'll surely wish they never had xenarthra.

xenarthra: a suborder or other division of Edentata comprising American anteaters, sloths, armadillos, etc.

Yellow Jacket

Let's talk about a wasp, the "yellow jacket" wasp, by name.
Though it's said to be a carnivore, that's not its claim to fame.
It feeds on other insects, from the fruit fly to the flea,
But it also has an appetite for bigger things — like me.

It is called a "social wasp," a term that seems a bit ironic.
An "antisocial wasp" would be much less oxymoronic,
For despite its lofty title and its vaunted social status,
It is readily apparent that all wasps of that sort hate us.

It is busy, as it buzzes 'round while we attend our garden,
And, being social, bites us and then says, "I beg your pardon."
While, clearly, it's observing the approved amenities,
It elicits, in the process, several choice obscenities.

That social wasp has proved to be carnivorous, however.
It may be social, but to tell the truth, it's not too clever.
It sits nibbling at my arm. However, little does it know
That in this world, it 's written, there's a quid for each pro quo.

Although it likes to nosh on *Homo sapiens*, for lunch,
I shall be laying plans for its demise, I have a hunch.
Because when all the t's are crossed and all the i's are dotted,
It is written that wasp is gonna end up being swatted.

Zebu

When it's summer and I'm sweating and my clothes are soaking wet
And I'm swatting at mosquitoes and by insects I'm beset,
Then I dream that I'm a zebu and by bugs I'm unaffected.
Though it's ninety-nine degrees outside, I'm cool and I'm collected.

For the zebu is a great big ox that's native to east Asia.
It is used for milk and meat. But there's one thing that will amaze ya'.
In addition to its size, all zebu experts are insistent
That to heat and to most insects, zebus seem to be resistant.

When I dream that I'm a zebu, you can see just where I'm at.
I'd be free of heat and insects. But there's just one caveat.
As a source of milk, I'd have no problem, but I have a hunch
I'd dread the thought of having someone munch on me for lunch.

zebu: a domestic ox in India and east Asia, with a large fleshy hump over the shoulders (a dewlap); the zebu has a marked resistance to heat and insects

Zeuglodon

The zeuglodon
Is gone.

That cetacean was last seen
In the epoch Eocene,
And today, there are no creatures zeuglodonic.
No one knows, to be precise,
What caused that whale's demise,
But it did not die from plagues like the bubonic.

Though fossil experts can't agree,
It is obvious to me
That their long teeth may have been why they are gone.
Since we're told they're "long in tooth"
(That means "old age," long past one's youth) —
That's what happened to the species *Zeuglodon*.

My theory, true, has few adherents,
About cetaceans' disappearance,
But no scientists have risen to refute it.
They are gone; that's undeniable.
But they might still be viable
If their teeth were, like my theory, firmly rooted.

zeuglodon: an extinct whale of the Eocene and Miocene epochs; a suborder
of cetacean characterized by long, slender teeth

Yak

If you are somewhere in Tibet
And you're looking for a snack,
A hearty source of protein
Is the woolly, hairy yak.

The yak is very useful
For its hair and hide and milk,
Much more beneficial
Than most others of his ilk

Of course, the yak is six feet tall,
Weighs half a ton and more,
So, to satisfy your hunger pangs,
Perhaps you should explore

Other avenues for protein.
If you're looking for a snack,
Seek out the nearest "golden arch,"
And forget about the yak.

yak: a large, long-haired wild ox of Tibet and elevated areas of central Asia

Xiphias

Mourners gathered at the casket,
Saying sad farewells to Dan,
Tears cascading down their faces,
As the minister began.

"Dan, angels wait on you, in Heaven.
Your good deeds are your memorial.
We grieve for your untimely fate,
Uniquely piscatorial.

"Neal, Dan's guide, said, 'Look, a xiphias!
A trophy fish! Jump in and spear it!'
So, fearless Dan donned mask and fins,
But just before he could get near it,

"The xiphias turned, swam straight at Dan,
And Dan was skewered. End of story.
Cried Neal, 'Oops! Dan, I just forgot.
Xiphias is a swordfish. Sorry!'

"So, let us rise and pray for Dan.
Neal sealed his fate, to be quite candid.
It's a lesson learned. You get the point —
That's why we're here today — 'cause Dan did."

Wallaroo — Who?

Wallaroo is a marsupial,
Like the Aussie kangaroo.
He's a cousin of the wallaby,
And there are others too.

All are genus *Macropus*
(In Greek, that means "big feet").
Wallaroo is *M. Robustus*,
'Cause he's big, though not too fleet.

He is also called the "euro,"
In the west-Australian ranges,
Which leads to some confusion
At their currency exchanges.

If you ask for euros at a bank,
Changing money could perplex us.
The clerk might ask, "Which euro, sir?
We have euros of both sexes."

There is more about the *Macropus*
That you might well give heed to,
Though, about this topic, you now know
More than you want or need to.

wallaroo: a gray animal, called the common wallaroo; in central and western
Australia, it is reddish and is known as the euro

Veery

Once upon a midnight dreary, as I pondered on the veery,
Huddled over many a weighty volume of Roget and more,
Out of nowhere came the notion: veery's habitat is ocean?
At a loss to solve that question, I decided to explore
Britannica from A to Z. Though over every page I'd pore,
From those volumes nothing more.

One time, I hypothecated that the veery had migrated
From the frozen tundra near Siberia's eastern shore.
That idea, too, died aborning, in the cold light of the morning,
Leaving me with other theories, some of them no less bizarre,
Theories which, to my amazement, I had not embraced before —
Writer's block and nothing more.

Though, in truth, Poe was no maven when it came to birds, his raven
Left his readers mesmerized and spread his fame from shore to shore.
So, like Poe, I focused on a certain kind of avifauna.
There, I came upon the veery — "Wilson's thrush," in avian lore.
Said the veery, "You will know me; I'm adorned with spots galore."
Spoke the veery nothing more.

veery: common American thrush; sometimes known as "Wilson's thrush," it
is light tawny-brown above, pale buff below

Urubu

Whence comest thou, odd urubu?
What or who or why are you?

Are you some sort of Third World king
Or perhaps a grand-chef offering?

Are you an old religious sect
Or an outmoded dialect?

What are you, urubu? High culture?
No, you're just a lowly vulture.

To the turkey buzzard you're related,
Although you're not as widely hated.

"Vulture," "buzzard" sound abhorrent,
But words like "urubu" just aren't.

It's likely you'd be more despisable
If you had a name more recognizable.

urubu: the black vulture

Terrapin

The tortoise and the terrapin
Zoologically are next of kin.
Confusion reigns about their name.
I'm almost sure that they're the same.

How clever of the terrapin —
He's born with neither gills nor fin
Yet swims much faster than he crawls,
And he's built so low, he seldom falls.

I marvel at the terrapin,
Who's wrapped in nature's thickest skin.
His is the perfect hiding place —
Ensconced within his carapace.

Yet how does the torpid terrapin,
When given to philanderin',
Connect up with the fairer sex,
When all that sticks out are their necks?

What happens to the terrapin
If the husband should come strolling in?
How can he beat a quick retreat
When he's not shifty on his feet?

When danger lurks, the terrapin
Just sits and pulls his noggin in,
While I, unless the day is won,
Would get up off my duff and run.

Perhaps that's why the terrapin
Is never known to laugh or grin.
Though I, from fate's blows, can recoup,
He's apt to wind up in the soup.

Springbok, Springbok

Springbok, springbok, give me your answer true.
Why just spring back? Is that all you can do?
Would it be terribly horrid
If, once, you would spring forw'd?
You'd be the first, and unrehearsed —
Never performed hitherto.

Springbok, springbok, South Africa's home to you.
You hunt and bring back a savory snack or two.
Your hopping is athletic,
But you would look pathetic
If you gained weight from what you ate.
It could well be the end of you.

Springbok, springbok, those calories you will rue.
Those snacks you bring back could add to your waistline, too.
When you're no longer thinnish,
Your leaping will diminish.
You'll look and feel like a tasty meal
For a tiger that lives near you.

springbok: a swift and graceful southern-African gazelle, noted for its
habit of springing lightly and suddenly into the air

Roebuck

The snow was falling without stopping,
And with Christmas just a month away,
The stag thought, "I must do some shopping,
Getting ready for the holiday."

Off he raced, past crowded stores,
Past Macy's, Saks, and Bloomingdale's,
Right through Sears's revolving doors,
With the store detective on his tail.

"Hey, you can't do your shopping here!
This is no zoo department store!
We don't sell clothing for a deer!"
And he led the stag back toward the door.

Said the stag, "You'll sing a different tune.
I always shop here. Furthermore,
You might just need a new job soon,
Because my family owns this store."

The guard laughed. "Hey, you're way off base!
Beat it, deer! Don't push your luck!"
"But my family really owns this place.
I'm a very *sear*ious roebuck."

roebuck: a male small European and Asiatic deer (roe deer), with erect, forked, cylindrical antlers; roe deer are known for their nimbleness and gracefulness

Quetzal?

In the land of Guatemala,
The quetzal's something like our dollar.
If you go there, you'll soon know what "quetzal" means —
It's the local legal tender.
So, if you are a big spender,
You should have a lot of quetzals in your jeans.

When in Cotzumalguapa,
Spending quetzals would be proper,
But there's more than just one meaning to that word.
The savvy visitor should know
"Quetzal" stands for more than dough.
It is also Guatemala's national bird.

Now, in Mexico you'll find
A quetzal of a different kind,
A bird for which they have a great affinity:
It's a truly noble quetzal,
With a two-foot tail that gets all
Flying insects buzzing in that bird's vicinity.

Just think: what could be odder
Than a Yucatan fly-swatter
That can keep one's hacienda free of pests?
And you wouldn't be regretting
Life without mosquito netting,
With your siestas having no unwelcome guests.

quetzal: a nonpasserine tropical bird with brilliant plumage; the national bird of Guatemala; also the monetary unit of Guatemala

Platypus

I have no use
For the platypus.
It isn't good to eat.

It's nose is broad,
It's tail is flat,
And, likewise, are its feet.

platypus: a semiaquatic egg-laying mammal; its name comes from the Greek words "platys" ("broad") and "pous" ("foot")

Ortolan

This page presents a lesson on
How one should eat the ortolan.
First, you hop aboard a plane that's Paris-bound.
There, you seek a proper venue,
Where ortolan is on the menu
And the chef who runs the place is world-renowned.

You'll be escorted to a table,
With a wine list *formidable*,
And the owner-chef emerges with his greeting.
"*Bon matin*," the chef will say.
"*Merci. Attendez, s'il vous plait*,"
Pointing to the little bird that you'll be eating.

If you're attentive, you'll now get
The bona fide French etiquette,
As he demonstrates the proper way to do it.
He puts three birds upon his plate,
And as you start to salivate,
He picks one up and slowly starts to chew it.

It isn't clear what he is doing,
Because he simply goes on chewing,
And he chews until the whole thing disappears.
"Those little bones! My gosh!" you shout.
"I didn't see you spit them out!"
"You must eat those little bones," he volunteers.

You gulp. Now comes the acid test.
The chef, now, slowly chews the rest.
And he chews on each bird, as you sit enthralled.
By now, you've started feeling ill.
But his molars keep on churning till —
Voilà! Those birds have vanished, bones and all.

That's how it's done, though you may doubt it.
But it's the truth, no bones about it.

ortolan: a small passerine bird (bunting) native to Europe and Africa; a
European delicacy

Noctiluca (*Noctiluca scintillans*)

You may find you're loath to loiter
When you start to reconnoiter
The ocean floor, because it's dark and scary.
But if you choose the right location,
You will have no trepidation
About your deep-blue-sea itinerary.

There's noctiluca — it's a flagellate
With long feelers that illuminate
The ocean with an eerie phosphorescence
That will brighten up *la mer*
Like the lights around Times Square
And relieve your apprehension by their presence.

They just float about, with ease,
Like Old Glory in the breeze.
It's a most unusual seaweed eccentricity,
And it's really quite exciting —
A kind of plant with built-in lighting,
With no generator for its electricity.

If you could harvest it, that's cool.
You'd phosphoresce your swimming pool.
Your underwater lighting you could jettison,
And when you pay your monthly bills,
There's one dream that it fulfills:
You could thumb your nose once monthly at Con Edison.

noctiluca (Noctiluca scintillans): a genus of marine flagellates that is unusually large and complexly structured; bioluminescent, they are responsible for the phenomenon known as the "red tide" and give off a spectacular phosphorescence at night

Mongoose

There are pitfalls in our language of which one should be aware.
If one goose and another goose make two geese, it seems fair
That the plural of the mongoose should be mongeese. *Au contraire.*

If you'll open up your *Webster's,* under "m," it introduces
The plural of the mongoose. There, one rapidly deduces
That when there's more than one mongoose, they must be called
   "mongooses."

And we run into another problem with the mother tongue.
If to some basic logic Noah Webster's book had clung,
A little mongoose ought to be "mongosling" when it's young.

One more semantic flaw exists that seems to raise my dander.
The world knows that the father of a gosling is a gander.
Why is it that a male mongoose is never a "mongander"?

Whatever it is called, it's an unlikely household pet.
In the Far East and the Middle East, the mongoose, a civet,
Has plats du jour of lizard eggs and poison snakes. And yet,

Though the mongoose ecologically appears to have some uses,
With that funny plural name, I'm sure it suffers some abuses.
Still, no matter what their role in life, they just remain mongooses.

mongoose: a viverrine found in India; a member of the civet family; small
and carnivorous, it attacks snakes

Loris

Oh, the loris is a stranger in our land.
There are two of them — nocturnal lemurs — and
Sri Lanka is where one of them resides
(In East India the other one abides).
But the loris is a stranger in our land.

Did the loris dwell among us heretofore?
Oh, there may be one or two in Baltimore,
But in zoos in each metropolis,
They aren't very populous.
Did the loris just ignore us on our shore?

So, if you would see a loris, board a plane
For Sri Lanka, where a few of them remain,
Or you could find a loris at
Its far East Indies habitat,
'Cause no lorises remain on our terrain.

Or just settle for a loris photographic
By subscribing to the *National Geographic*.

loris: either of two species of slow-moving nocturnal lemurs

Krait

I don't want to meet a cobra,
      Drunk or sobra,
But I'd be more devastated
      To see a krait uncrated,
Since the krait is much more venomous
      And has, for me, an animus.
I would just say, "Bye-bye, krait,"
      And absquatulate.

krait: a brightly banded, extremely venomous snake of Pakistan, India, and Southeast Asia

Jaguar

My neighbor has a jaguar, so I thought I'd buy one too.
In fact, we have the only jaguars on our avenue.
His jaguar's sleek and tawny and is beautifully spotted.
I wash my Jaguar weekly, and it's spotless since I got it.

He says his jaguar's sleek and indisputably more swift,
But mine is just as well designed, with automatic shift.
His jaguar is so fast that you can lose it in a forest.
Mine is just as speedy, if the radar would ignore us.

If his is stopped for speeding, it need not appear in court.
The police just think that chasing him is something of a sport.
But if my Jaguar's speeding, the police do more than blame it.
It's put in storage, by the court, until I pay to claim it.

His feeds on carbohydrates and the rodent population.
Mine lives on hydrocarbons, with high-octane stimulation.
The upkeep on my neighbor's jaguar is, you might say, minimal,
While insurance, yearly, on my Jaguar borders on the criminal.

So, if you are in the market for a jaguar of some sort
And you think that raising wildcats is a jolly sort of sport,
My neighbor's jaguar would not be the ideal household pet.
Most people stay as far away from it as they can get.

Though we recognize the jaguar as a product of the Lord,
While mine is only one of several thousand made by Ford,
The bottom line is that your friendly jaguar's appetite
Could mean that you might wind up as his bedtime snack one night.

Ibis

A canticle for ibises is proper,
For, in Florida, they often come a cropper.
     Although graceful, it's a slow bird,
     And another bird, the snowbird,
Wages war on ibises, and that's improper.

They invade the ibis native habitat,
The club golf course, but there's more to it than that.
     They use myriad devices
     To correct their hooks and slices
(All the lessons from the pros have fallen flat).

To suggest the snowbird's evil — no, we daren't.
It is simply that their aim is often errant.
     They're not ibis-cidal, really.
     They're just out there, swinging freely.
If you watch them on the fairway, that's apparent.

Every club becomes a deadly catapult.
When they're used, no good can come as a result.
     The ball's course is unintended,
     But the ibis's life is ended —
A misguided missile, not the missile's fault.

So, let's say a prayer for that departed bird,
Felled in a way it would not have preferred,
     Victim of a flying missile —
     A sad lesson from which this'll
Penalize the hacker just one stroke, we've heard.

ibis: a wading bird related to the heron but distinguished by a long, slender, downwardly curved bill

Hyrax

"There's a rabbit in my yard!" my neighbor shouted.
He thinks that it's a rabbit, but I doubt it.
Its feet are padded, so it's soil-resistant,
And its little tail is almost nonexistent.

It's a hyrax. It looks strange to you, albeit
It is probable "you'll know it when you see it."
With its little legs and tail that's rudimentary,
It is not a bunny; that is elementary.

You'd think it has a nasty disposition
If you saw that little creature's strange dentition.
Its canine teeth are ratlike (they can gnaw some),
And its molars look like rhino's molars — awesome!

So, if you're a rabbit lover and astute
And what you're looking at is harelike and it's cute,
It is possibly a hyrax, so don't pet it,
'Cause if it nibbles on your fingers, you'll regret it.

One thing that bugs me so I can't relax is
A worrisome detail about hyraxes:
Is "hyraxes" the accepted plural word,
Or is "hyraces" the form that is preferred?

Goat Antelope (Chamois)

Would you wash your car with an antelope
Or use a goat to polish brass?
Would you hang an antelope out to dry
Or use a goat to demist glass?

It all sounds so nonsensical,
But it is really not bizarre.
The chamois is an antelope,
Looks like a goat. So there you are!

Fitch

Let's say you chance upon a fitch
While you're tramping through the quitch,*
And all at once, you get the itch
To use the fitch to make you rich.

The fitch would occupy a niche
As a novelty fur, which,
Even though it might be kitsch,
Could attract the idle rich.

But before you cut and stitch
All those flitches of the fitch,
There could be one little hitch
That could dissipate that itch.

Lest you suffer from that glitch,
Toss that fitch into a ditch,
For you have trapped a polecat, which
Is known in Europe as a "fitch."

*quitch: a rapidly spreading grass; also called "twitch" or "witch grass"

Eft

If, orthographically, you're deft,
Just drop the letter "l" from "left."
What's left? The eft.

What's an eft? If you're astute,
And you'll join in the pursuit,
You'll find the eft is just a newt.

Through that phylum now meander.
It's there in print, just take a gander.
The newt is just a salamander,

And you need not be a wizard
To learn (just search from A to izzard)
That the salamander is a lizard,

A first cousin of the croc,
Of alligator-family stock.
Now, if you'll roll back the clock

To countless epochs gone before,
You'll find the dreaded dinosaur
Was the croc's progenitor.

So, if your reasoning is deft,
The one conclusion that is left
Is that the dinosaur and eft

Are related rather closely.
(I should say they're cousins, mostly,
If the kinship's looked at grossly.)

Summing up, to be succinct,
Although by ancestry they're linked,
The eft, though small, is less extinct.

Drill

There are several "drill"s in *Webster's*
That one quickly recognizes.
There's the drill that's used for making holes,
And there are army exercises.

However, there are other drills
You may not see around you.
There's a little snail that's called a drill,
And there's a drill that will astound you.

Be sure your camera's ready
As your safari is pursuin'.
The drill that lives in Africa —
There, the drill is a baboon.

Cachalot

If you're the sort of person who's addicted to the rare,
You will love the cachalot, there's no denying.
But before you shop around to see where you can find a pair,
Perhaps you ought to know just what you're buying.

The cachalot's a mammal — it's a whale, to be exact.
It is not what you would call a cuddly pet.
You'd have to board it in your swimming pool, and that's a fact.
That could possibly discourage you, and yet

If you would like to own some sort of creature that's unique,
The cachalot is sure to hit the spot.
But you should be forewarned: if that's the trophy that you seek,
You'd better be equipped with cash — a lot.

Bandicoot

There's a bandicoot "A" and a bandicoot "B."
"A" bandicoot isn't "B"'s brother.
The two can't lay claim to the same family tree.
They've not even met one another.

Bandicoot "A" is an Indian rodent.
His home is in sewers and gutters.
On various human tidbits, "A" is dotin';
They're his choice plats du jour in Calcutta.

Bandicoot "B" is a native Australian.
He's really a rabbit. Moreover,
His diet is nothing like bandicoot "A"'s;
In fact, it's just insects and clover.

I think I would rather meet "B," from down under,
Than bandicoot "A," from up over.

Armadillo

When you think of the steel armor on the army's Sherman tank,
It is possible that it's the armadillo you can thank.
Its body is encased in little rounded horny plates,
Ossified to form a shield that nothing penetrates.
With such an armored carapace, it is to be expected
That its head and tail and all four limbs are equally protected.

Armed like that, the armadillo ought to be supreme.
But in the kingdom of the beasts, things aren't what they seem.
The armadillo's rather slow, not given to adventures.
One reason is they have no teeth and no armadillo dentures.
They come out after dark, to seek for food among the plants,
But all they seem to do is root around for bugs and ants.

You may wonder why the Lord put armadillos here on earth
(What could their role in nature be, to demonstrate their worth?) —
A conundrum that you're free to solve if you are so inclined.
But whatever possibilities are apt to come to mind,
Of one thing you can be certain: when you see the armadillo,
He wasn't put on earth for you to use him as a pillow.

Biographical Note

Ben Milder, a native of St. Louis, is the author of more than a thousand light-verse poems, written over the past fifty years. In 1979, his book *The Fine Art of Prescribing Glasses Without Making a Spectacle of Yourself*, a medical text laced with light verse, won the American Medical Writers Association's AMMY award for Best New Book of the Year in Medical and Applied Sciences. Milder's work is represented in the anthology *The Best of Medical Humor* and has been published in the *Palm Beach Post*, *St. Louis Post-Dispatch*, *Milwaukee Sentinel*, *Journal of Irreproducible Results*, *Light*, *Pharos*, *The Critic*, *Long Island Night Life*, and numerous medical journals.

Other Poetry and Short Fictions Available from Time Being Books

EDWARD BOCCIA
No Matter How Good the Light Is: Poems by a Painter

LOUIS DANIEL BRODSKY
You Can't Go Back, Exactly
The Thorough Earth
Four and Twenty Blackbirds Soaring
Mississippi Vistas: Volume One of *A Mississippi Trilogy*
Falling from Heaven: Holocaust Poems of a Jew and a Gentile *(Brodsky and Heyen)*
Forever, for Now: Poems for a Later Love
Mistress Mississippi: Volume Three of *A Mississippi Trilogy*
A Gleam in the Eye: Poems for a First Baby
Gestapo Crows: Holocaust Poems
The Capital Café: Poems of Redneck, U.S.A.
Disappearing in Mississippi Latitudes: Volume Two of *A Mississippi Trilogy*
Paper-Whites for Lady Jane: Poems of a Midlife Love Affair
The Complete Poems of Louis Daniel Brodsky: Volume One, 1963-1967
Three Early Books of Poems by Louis Daniel Brodsky, 1967-1969: *The Easy Philosopher*, *"A Hard Coming of It" and Other Poems*, and *The Foul Rag-and-Bone Shop*
The Eleventh Lost Tribe: Poems of the Holocaust
Toward the Torah, Soaring: Poems of the Renascence of Faith
Yellow Bricks *(short fictions)*
Catchin' the Drift o' the Draft *(short fictions)*
This Here's a Merica *(short fictions)*
Voice Within the Void: Poems of *Homo supinus*
Leaky Tubs *(short fictions)*
Shadow War: A Poetic Chronicle of September 11 and Beyond, Volume One
The Complete Poems of Louis Daniel Brodsky: Volume Two, 1967-1976
Shadow War: A Poetic Chronicle of September 11 and Beyond, Volume Two
Shadow War: A Poetic Chronicle of September 11 and Beyond, Volume Three
Shadow War: A Poetic Chronicle of September 11 and Beyond, Volume Four
Shadow War: A Poetic Chronicle of September 11 and Beyond, Volume Five
Rated Xmas *(short fictions)*

HARRY JAMES CARGAS *(editor)*
Telling the Tale: A Tribute to Elie Wiesel on the Occasion of His 65th Birthday — Essays, Reflections, and Poems

JUDITH CHALMER
Out of History's Junk Jar: Poems of a Mixed Inheritance

(866) 840-4334
http://www.timebeing.com

GERALD EARLY

How the War in the Streets Is Won: Poems on the Quest of Love and Faith

GARY FINCKE

Blood Ties: Working-Class Poems

ALBERT GOLDBARTH

A Lineage of Ragpickers, Songpluckers, Elegiasts & Jewelers: Selected Poems
   of Jewish Family Life, 1973-1995

ROBERT HAMBLIN

From the Ground Up: Poems of One Southerner's Passage to Adulthood

WILLIAM HEYEN

Erika: Poems of the Holocaust
Falling from Heaven: Holocaust Poems of a Jew and a Gentile *(Brodsky and Heyen)*
Pterodactyl Rose: Poems of Ecology
Ribbons: The Gulf War — A Poem
The Host: Selected Poems, 1965–1990

TED HIRSCHFIELD

German Requiem: Poems of the War and the Atonement of a Third Reich Child

VIRGINIA V. JAMES HLAVSA

Waking October Leaves: Reanimations by a Small-Town Girl

RODGER KAMENETZ

The Missing Jew: New and Selected Poems
Stuck: Poems Midlife

NORBERT KRAPF

Somewhere in Southern Indiana: Poems of Midwestern Origins
Blue-Eyed Grass: Poems of Germany

ADRIAN C. LOUIS

Blood Thirsty Savages

(866) 840-4334
http://www.timebeing.com

LEO LUKE MARCELLO

Nothing Grows in One Place Forever: Poems of a Sicilian American

GARDNER McFALL

The Pilot's Daughter

JOSEPH MEREDITH

Hunter's Moon: Poems from Boyhood to Manhood

BEN MILDER

The Good Book Says . . . : Light Verse to Illuminate the Old Testament
The Good Book Also Says . . . : Numerous Humorous Poems Inspired by the
   New Testament
Love Is Funny, Love Is Sad

CHARLES MUÑOZ

Fragments of a Myth: Modern Poems on Ancient Themes

MICHEAL O'SIADHAIL

The Gossamer Wall: Poems in Witness to the Holocaust

JOSEPH STANTON

Imaginary Museum: Poems on Art